THE WINNING MONEY MINDSET

Shifting Your Financial Paradigms in a way that will change your life

Mitchell Larry

WHY THIS BOOK

"The Winning Money Mindset: Shifting Your Financial Paradigms in a Way That Will Change Your Life" stands out for several compelling reasons that make it a must-read for anyone looking to transform their financial situation. Here are special reasons why people should choose or buy this book:

1. **Unique Psychological Insight**: This book delves deep into the psychological aspects of financial decision-making, offering readers a unique perspective on how their thoughts and beliefs about money can shape their financial reality. It's not just about managing money; it's about understanding the mindset behind every financial decision.

2. **Practical and Actionable Strategies**: Unlike many other books that offer vague advice, "The Winning Money Mindset" provides practical, actionable strategies that readers can immediately implement to start seeing a positive change in their financial life. These strategies are designed to be adaptable to any financial situation, ensuring everyone can benefit.

3. **Personal Transformation Stories**: The book includes inspiring stories of real people who have successfully shifted their financial paradigms and achieved remarkable financial freedom.

These stories not only motivate but also demonstrate the effectiveness of the book's teachings in real-life scenarios.

4. **Expert Authorship**: Written by an expert in the field of personal finance and self-help, the book is backed by years of research, personal experience, and success stories. This expertise ensures the advice is not only sound but also proven to work.

5. **Comprehensive Financial Education**: From budgeting to investing, the book covers all aspects of personal finance, making it a comprehensive guide for anyone looking to improve their financial literacy. It's designed to be the only book you'll ever need to read on the subject.

6. **Mindset Shifts for Long-term Success**: The book emphasizes the importance of long-term mindset shifts over quick fixes. It's focused on sustainable financial health, teaching readers how to develop habits and mindsets that will benefit them for the rest of their lives.

7. **Interactive Exercises**: Throughout the book, readers will find interactive exercises designed to help them apply the concepts in real time. These exercises encourage self-reflection and personal growth, making the reading experience both engaging and transformative.

8. **Accessibility**: "The Winning Money Mindset" is written in an accessible, jargon-free language, making it suitable for financial novices and experts alike. This accessibility ensures that anyone can understand and apply the book's teachings.

By choosing "The Winning Money Mindset," readers are not just buying a book; they are investing in a life-changing journey towards financial enlightenment and empowerment.

Table of Contents

Introduction

In the heart of a bustling city, beneath the towering skyscrapers and amidst the ceaseless rhythm of daily life, lived Joe. Joe's story was not unlike many others, a narrative woven with dreams, struggles, and the relentless pursuit of happiness. However, what set Joe apart was an unshakeable feeling of being trapped in a financial maze, constantly running but never finding the exit to true financial freedom. This is where our journey begins, with "The Winning Money Mindset: Shifting Your Financial Paradigms in a Way That Will Change Your Life," a book that would soon transform Joe's world in ways unimaginable.

Joe, a mid-level manager at a technology firm, had achieved what many would consider the markers of success: a steady job, a comfortable apartment, and a social life filled with friends and laughter. Yet, beneath this veneer of achievement lay a persistent anxiety about money. Despite earning a respectable salary, Hoe lived paycheck to paycheck, ensnared in a cycle of debt and deferred dreams. Savings were a concept Alex admired from afar, and investing was a language yet to be learned. The future was a horizon marred by financial clouds, a stark contrast to the life of abundance Joe had always envisioned.

It was on a crisp autumn morning, with the leaves painting the city in hues of fire, that Joe's friend, Jordan, introduced "The Winning Money Mindset." Over coffee, Jordan shared tales of transformation and enlightenment, of how this book had reshaped their understanding of wealth and propelled them toward financial liberation. Skeptical yet intrigued, Joe began the journey, unaware that the pages of this book would soon become the compass guiding them out of the financial labyrinth.

Chapter One revealed the root of Joe's financial conundrum: a mindset molded by a childhood of scarcity and caution, where money was the perennial guest that left too soon. The book prompted Joe to unearth these deep-seated beliefs, to confront them with the raw honesty of a soul seeking change. It was uncomfortable, confronting the shadows of the past, but within these shadows lay the keys to liberation.

As Joe delved deeper into "The Winning Money Mindset," each chapter unfolded like a map, revealing pathways previously obscured by fear and misunderstanding. Chapter Two, "The Psychology of Money," was a revelation. It spoke of cognitive biases and emotional spending, concepts that resonated with Joe's experiences. The book did not merely diagnose; it offered remedies, practical strategies to rewire the brain's approach to money, turning every decision from an emotional impulse to a strategic step toward prosperity.

With each page turned, Joe embarked on a transformative journey. The chapters on setting financial goals, building knowledge, and mastering money management became the milestones of progress. The exercises and real-life stories interspersed throughout the book were not just theoretical musings but actionable wisdom that Joe applied, slowly but surely, reconstructing their financial life from the ground up.

"The Art of Earning More" was a chapter that struck a particular chord. Joe had long resigned to the belief that their income was a fixed star in the financial galaxy, immovable and defined by the whims of the job market. The book challenged this notion, illuminating the myriad ways to augment income, from honing in-demand skills to venturing into the world of side hustles. It was a call to action that Alex answered with newfound zeal, exploring avenues of income that once seemed unreachable.

Investing, once a realm shrouded in mystery, became accessible through "Investing Wisely for Long-Term Growth." The book demystified stocks, bonds, and real estate, presenting them not as gambles but as calculated decisions aligned with Joe's financial goals. With each investment, Joe felt a step closer to the future they had dreamt of, a future where financial clouds gave way to clear skies.

Yet, it was not just about accumulating wealth. "Protecting Your Wealth" taught Joe the importance of safeguarding this newfound prosperity through insurance, estate planning, and tax efficiency. The book emphasized that true financial wisdom lay not just in earning and investing but in ensuring that wealth endured through life's unpredictabilities.

As the chapters of "The Winning Money Mindset" unfolded, so did the chapters of Joe's life. The transformation was not overnight, nor was it easy. There were setbacks and moments of doubt, times when the old mindset threatened to reclaim its territory. But with the book as a guide, Joe persevered, applying its lessons with diligence and faith.

Today, Joe stands at the precipice of a new chapter, one not written by circumstance but by choice. The financial maze that once seemed inescapable now lies behind, a testament to a journey of courage, learning, and growth. "The Winning Money Mindset" was more than a book; it was a beacon of hope, a mentor, and a friend that walked alongside Joe on the path to financial freedom.

This story, while unique to Joe, is universal in its message. It speaks to the power of mindset, the courage to confront and reshape deeply ingrained beliefs, and the transformative journey that follows. "The Winning Money Mindset" is not just about financial education; it's about financial emancipation, about shifting paradigms in a way that changes lives.

As we leave Joe to embark on this new chapter, we invite you, the reader, to reflect on your own financial journey. Where do you stand in your financial maze? Are you ready to take the first step toward your transformation? "The Winning Money Mindset" awaits, ready to guide you from the confines of financial uncertainty to the open spaces of financial freedom and prosperity. The journey is yours to begin.

Welcoming the Reader

Welcome, Dear Reader,

Congratulations on embarking on one of the most transformative journeys of your life with "The Winning Money Mindset: Shifting Your Financial Paradigms in a Way That Will Change Your Life." This book is not just a collection of pages; it's a gateway to a new way of thinking, a new way of living, and most importantly, a new way of managing and understanding your finances.

You're about to dive into a comprehensive guide designed to reshape your relationship with money. Whether you're struggling with financial anxiety, seeking to break free from the paycheck-to-paycheck cycle, or aiming to elevate your financial game to new heights, you've made the right choice. This book is for those who dare to dream of financial independence and are ready to take actionable steps to make those dreams a reality.

We've crafted this journey to be both enlightening and practical, blending psychological insights with actionable financial strategies. Each chapter is structured to build upon the last, creating a solid foundation of knowledge that will empower you to take control of your financial destiny. Through a combination of theory, real-life success stories, and interactive exercises, you'll discover how to transform your money mindset from the ground up.

Here's what you can expect:

- **Deep Understanding**: Gain insights into the psychological barriers that have been holding you back and learn how to overcome them.
- **Actionable Advice**: Receive practical, straightforward strategies to improve your financial habits, increase your income, and grow your wealth.
- **Real-Life Inspiration**: Be motivated by stories of real individuals who have successfully shifted their financial paradigms and achieved financial freedom.
- **Interactive Exercises**: Engage with exercises designed to apply the concepts you're learning directly to your life, ensuring you're not just reading but actively participating in your financial transformation.

This book is more than just a read; it's an experience. It's an invitation to challenge your existing beliefs about money, to explore new possibilities, and to take bold steps towards a future where financial worries are a thing of the past. As you turn each page, remember that every word has been carefully chosen to guide you, inspire you, and ultimately, help you to unlock the door to your financial freedom.

So, dear reader, as you prepare to begin this journey, we invite you to open your mind, ready your pen for notes and exercises, and embrace the transformation that awaits. Your financial future starts now. Welcome to "The Winning Money Mindset."

With warmest regards,

Michell Larry

Author of "The Winning Money Mindset"

Overview of the Money Mindset Shift

Embarking on "The Winning Money Mindset" journey, you're about to explore the profound transformation that awaits when you shift your financial paradigms. This shift is not merely about changing how you budget, save, or invest; it's about altering the very fabric of your relationship with money. It's a transformation that moves you from a state of financial survival to a state of financial thriving. Let's delve into what this shift entails and what it promises for your life.

From Scarcity to Abundance

Many of us are tethered to a scarcity mindset, a belief that there is never enough. This book will guide you away from this limiting belief, toward an abundance mindset where opportunities for wealth and growth are seen as ever-present and accessible. This fundamental shift will change how you view money, opening doors to new possibilities for wealth creation.

Reactive to Proactive Financial Habits

The journey from being reactive—constantly dealing with financial emergencies without a plan—to adopting a proactive stance on your finances is crucial. You'll learn to anticipate future needs and plan accordingly, transforming your financial decisions from spontaneous reactions to informed, strategic choices.

Fear to Confidence

Fear often governs financial decisions, leading to missed opportunities and a lack of growth. As you shift your money mindset, you'll replace fear with confidence, empowering you to make bold decisions that align with your financial goals and aspirations.

Ignorance to Knowledge

Ignorance about personal finance can be a significant barrier to financial freedom. This book is your bridge to knowledge, offering you the tools, concepts, and strategies necessary to navigate the complex world of finance with ease and understanding.

Isolation to Community

Many people manage their finances in isolation, viewing money as a taboo topic. This shift encourages breaking down those barriers, fostering a sense of community where learning and growth are shared experiences. Through stories and shared wisdom, you'll realize you're not alone on this journey.

Short-term Gratification to Long-term Vision

The allure of instant gratification often detracts from our long-term financial health. "The Winning Money Mindset" emphasizes the importance of a long-term vision, teaching you to prioritize lasting wealth and security over fleeting pleasures.

Victimhood to Empowerment

Shifting your money mindset means moving away from seeing yourself as a victim of circumstances to recognizing your power to shape your financial destiny. This book will equip you with the mindset and tools to take control, making you the architect of your financial future.

What This Shift Means for You

Imagine a life where financial worries are replaced with financial wisdom, where every financial decision propels you closer to your dreams. This is the promise of "The Winning Money Mindset." Through this shift, you'll discover:

- How to cultivate a deep sense of financial peace and security.
- Strategies to grow your wealth in ways that align with your values and life goals.
- The freedom that comes from breaking the cycle of living paycheck to paycheck.
- The joy of using your financial resources to not only enrich your life but also to make a positive impact on the world around you.

As you turn the pages of this book, keep in mind that the journey ahead is one of transformation and growth. The shift in mindset you're about to undertake is the first step toward a life of financial freedom and abundance. Welcome to the beginning of your new financial paradigm.

How This Book Will Change Your Life

Embarking on the journey through "The Winning Money Mindset" is more than just reading a book; it's initiating a profound transformation in your life. This guide is meticulously designed to not only change how you think about money but also to revolutionize your approach to achieving financial freedom and prosperity. Here's a glimpse into the transformative power of this book and how it promises to reshape your life.

Shifts Your Perspective on Money

The core of this transformation begins with a fundamental shift in how you perceive money. By challenging and reshaping your deep-seated beliefs and fears about wealth, this book helps you move from a scarcity mindset, where money is a source of anxiety, to an abundance mindset, where money is viewed as a tool for creating the life you desire. This shift in perspective opens the door to new possibilities, enabling you to approach financial decisions with confidence and clarity.

Empowers You with Financial Literacy

Knowledge is power, especially when it comes to managing your finances. "The Winning Money Mindset" demystifies the complex world of personal finance, from budgeting and saving to investing and wealth protection. By providing you with a solid foundation of financial knowledge, this book empowers you to make informed decisions that align with your goals and aspirations, setting the stage for long-term financial success.

Instills Proactive Financial Habits

Gone are the days of reactive financial decisions and living paycheck to paycheck. This book guides you through the process of developing proactive financial habits, teaching you how to plan ahead, set actionable goals, and create a budget that works for you. These habits are the building blocks of financial stability and growth, ensuring that you're always moving forward on your path to financial freedom.

Encourages a Holistic Approach to Wealth

"The Winning Money Mindset" recognizes that true wealth extends beyond financial figures. It encourages a holistic approach to wealth that includes your well-being, relationships, and personal fulfillment. By aligning your financial goals with your values and dreams, this book helps you create a life that is not only financially prosperous but also rich in happiness and purpose.

Provides Tools for Overcoming Financial Challenges

Life is unpredictable, and financial setbacks are part of the journey. However, this book equips you with the resilience and tools needed to overcome these challenges. Through practical advice, strategies, and real-life examples, you'll learn how to navigate through tough financial times and emerge stronger on the other side.

Fosters a Sense of Community and Support

Financial transformation can be a daunting journey to undertake alone. "The Winning Money Mindset" fosters a sense of community and shared learning, reminding you that you're not alone in this journey. The stories of transformation and success within its pages serve as a source of inspiration and support, encouraging you to share your own experiences and learn from others.

Leads to a Life of Financial Freedom and Joy

Ultimately, the journey through "The Winning Money Mindset" leads to a destination of financial freedom and joy. Imagine a life where financial worries no longer dictate your choices, where you have the freedom to pursue your passions, support your loved ones, and contribute to causes you care about. This book is your roadmap to such a life, guiding you through each step with wisdom, compassion, and practical advice.

"The Winning Money Mindset" is more than a book; it's a catalyst for profound change. By embracing the lessons within its pages, you're not just improving your financial situation; you're transforming your life. You'll emerge from this journey with a new perspective on money, empowered with the knowledge and habits necessary for achieving lasting financial success and happiness. Welcome to the first day of your transformed life.

Chapter 1: Unveiling Your Current Financial Paradigm

"Money is a terrible master but an excellent servant." - P.T. Barnum

In the labyrinth of life, your financial beliefs are the compass guiding your every turn. Yet, so few of us question the origin or validity of this compass. Is it leading us to a treasure trove of prosperity and security, or are we being directed towards a mirage in the desert of financial instability? This chapter is the beginning of a quest—a quest to uncover the map of your financial beliefs, understand the terrain shaped by your upbringing, and recalibrate your compass through self-assessment. This is not just about discovering where you are on the map; it's about deciding where you truly want to be.

Understanding Your Financial Beliefs

Every decision you make about money—how you earn it, spend it, save it, invest it, or even give it away—is rooted in your financial beliefs. These beliefs are the silent narrators of your financial story, often whispering so subtly in the back of your mind that you don't even realize they're there. Yet, they are powerful beyond measure, capable of propelling you towards abundance or anchoring you in scarcity.

Your financial beliefs did not appear out of thin air. They were formed, molded, and etched into your psyche through years of observation, experience, and education. From the first coin you held in your tiny palm to the first paycheck that landed in your bank account, every moment has been a brick in the foundation of your financial paradigm.

On one end of the spectrum, there are those who view money as a source of endless opportunities—a tool that unlocks the door to their dreams. On the opposite end, some see money as a constant source of anxiety and fear, an elusive butterfly always just out of reach. Where do you stand on this spectrum? Recognizing this is the first step towards financial transformation.

The Impact of Your Upbringing on Your Money Mindset

The roots of your financial beliefs run deep, entwined with the memories of your upbringing. The way your family approached money, the conversations that danced around the dinner table, the financial highs and lows—every moment was a lesson in the school of financial thought.

Every family has its own financial culture, a set of beliefs, practices, and attitudes towards money that is passed down through generations. For some, this culture is one of thrift and saving for the proverbial rainy day. For others, it's about living in the moment, with little thought for tomorrow. Reflecting on your family's financial culture can reveal a lot about your current financial habits and attitudes.

Awareness is the first step towards change. If the financial culture of your upbringing is not serving your aspirations, it's time to break the cycle. This doesn't mean discarding everything you've learned; rather, it's about keeping what works and rewriting what doesn't. Your financial future is not destined to be a mirror of the past; it can be whatever you choose to make of it.

Self-Assessment: Identifying Your Financial Habits and Beliefs

The most powerful tool at your disposal is self-reflection. Taking a deep dive into your financial habits and beliefs can be both enlightening and daunting. This self-assessment is not about judging yourself; it's about understanding yourself.

Start by mapping out your financial behaviors. How do you react to money coming in? What's your first instinct when you face unexpected expenses? How do you approach saving and investing? These questions are not trivial; they are the threads that weave the fabric of your financial life.

Behind every financial behavior is a belief. Perhaps you spend impulsively because you believe you deserve to enjoy the fruits of your labor. Maybe you hoard every penny out of fear that it might someday run out. Understanding the beliefs behind your behaviors is key to transforming them.

Armed with the insights from your self-assessment, you are now at the threshold of a new financial paradigm. This is where the journey truly begins. It's time to chart a course towards a financial mindset that aligns with your values, goals, and dreams. The path may not be easy, but the treasures that await are worth every step.

As we delve into the depths of understanding your financial beliefs, exploring the impact of your upbringing, and embarking on the crucial self-assessment, remember: this is more than a chapter in a book. It's the first chapter in the new story of your financial life—a story where you are the author, and abundance is the theme. Let's turn the page and begin.

Self-Reflection Questions

1. What is the earliest memory you have of money, and how does that memory influence your current financial behaviors? Reflect on the emotions and lessons tied to this memory. Understanding this can shed light on deep-seated beliefs about money that may be guiding your financial decisions today.

_____

_____

_____

_____

_____

2. Identify a financial habit you inherited from your family. Do you see this habit as beneficial or detrimental to your financial well-being? This question encourages you to dissect your financial practices, distinguishing between those that serve your goals and those that may be holding you back.

_____

_____

_____

_____

_____

3. When faced with a financial decision, what emotions typically arise? Are these emotions helpful or hindering? By recognizing the emotional responses you have towards money, you can start to see how they might influence your financial choices, potentially steering you towards or away from sound financial health.

_____

_____

_____

_____

_____

4. What is one financial belief you hold that you now recognize as limiting? How did this belief come to be, and what steps can you take to challenge it? This question prompts you to confront and question a limiting belief, setting the stage for you to rewrite it into a more empowering narrative.

_____

5. Reflecting on your current financial situation, what is one change you can make that aligns more closely with your ideal financial paradigm? This practical question urges you to not only identify but also commit to a specific action that will move you closer to your financial goals.

Chapter Summary

In Chapter 1, "Unveiling Your Current Financial Paradigm," we embark on a journey of self-discovery, peeling back the layers to reveal the foundational beliefs and habits that shape our financial realities. Beginning with an exploration of our financial beliefs, we delve into how these perceptions of money—whether as a source of opportunity or anxiety—govern our financial decisions. We then examine the profound impact our upbringing has on our money mindset, recognizing that our family's financial culture has instilled in us certain habits and attitudes towards money.

Through a process of self-assessment, we are encouraged to map out our financial behaviors and the underlying beliefs that drive them. This reflective exercise is not about self-judgment but about gaining clarity and understanding, providing us with the insights needed to initiate a transformative shift in our financial paradigm.

The chapter concludes by offering self-reflection questions, designed to deepen our personal understanding and to prompt actionable change. These questions serve as a bridge between insight and action, guiding us to reevaluate our financial beliefs and habits in the light of our newfound knowledge.

As we close this chapter, we stand at the threshold of transformation. Armed with a deeper understanding of our financial beliefs and their origins, we are poised to rewrite our financial story. This is not just the end of a chapter but the beginning of a new, empowering journey towards financial freedom and prosperity.

Chapter 2: The Psychology of Money

"Money is a mirror that reflects our deepest fears and greatest aspirations."
- Unknown

Money, in its essence, is neutral. It's a tool, a medium of exchange, a way to measure value. Yet, the feelings, behaviors, and decisions surrounding money are anything but neutral. They are deeply embedded in our psyche, influenced by a myriad of factors that shape our financial destiny. This chapter delves into the complex world of our financial psyche, exploring how our mindset affects our financial decisions, the role of cognitive biases in shaping our financial behavior, and the path to forging a positive relationship with money.

How Your Mindset Affects Your Financial Decisions

Our journey begins with an exploration of the landscape of our financial mindset. It's the lens through which we view our financial world, colored by experiences, beliefs, and emotions. This lens can either distort our financial vision, leading us down paths of missed opportunities and financial pitfalls, or it can clarify our view, guiding us towards informed decisions and financial prosperity.

The financial mindset is rooted in the deepest corners of our psyche, shaped by the stories we've heard, the experiences we've endured, and the lessons we've learned. It's a complex amalgamation of our past, our hopes for the future, and the realities of our present.

Our first encounters with money during childhood set the stage for our financial mindset. The attitudes and behaviors modeled by our caregivers become the scripts we unconsciously follow. For some, money was a source of conflict or scarcity, breeding anxiety and a scarcity mindset. For others, money was abundant but perhaps tied to notions of worth or love, intertwining financial success with self-esteem.

Beyond the family unit, culture and society at large play significant roles in shaping our financial mindset. Societal norms dictate what success looks like, often tying it closely to financial achievement. Cultural narratives around money, such as the valorization of self-made success or the virtue of frugality, further color our financial decisions.

The financial mindset manifests most vividly in our approach to risk and decision-making. Those with a growth mindset, who view challenges as opportunities for learning and growth, are more likely to embrace financial risks as pathways to potential reward. Conversely, those with a fixed mindset, who see their abilities and circumstances as static, may shy away from financial risks, potentially stunting their financial growth.

Recognizing the power of mindset in financial decision-making is the first step towards transformation. By acknowledging the roots of our financial beliefs, we can begin to question and reshape them. This process isn't about discarding our past but about understanding its influence on us and consciously choosing which beliefs to carry forward and which to reframe.

As we embark on this journey of uncovering and transforming our financial mindset, remember that change is a process, not a destination. It requires patience, persistence, and a willingness to confront uncomfortable truths. But the rewards of this journey are immeasurable, leading not only to better financial decisions but to a deeper understanding of ourselves and our place in the financial world.

In the following sections, we'll explore the specific cognitive biases that skew our financial decision-making and outline strategies for cultivating a positive relationship with money, further equipping you with the tools needed to reshape your financial destiny.

Cognitive Biases and Financial Decisions

In the intricate dance of financial decision-making, our minds often lead with steps influenced by cognitive biases. These biases are the psychological tendencies that cause us to deviate from rational judgment, leading us down paths of error in our thinking and, consequently, in our financial decisions. Understanding these biases is crucial for navigating the financial landscape with clarity and purpose.

Imagine you're buying a car. The first price you see sets an "anchor," and all subsequent prices are judged relative to this anchor. This bias affects not just purchasing decisions but also our financial expectations and investments. Recognizing this bias involves questioning the first piece of financial information we encounter, asking ourselves if it's truly reflective of value or merely an arbitrary anchor.

We love to be right. So much so, that we often seek out information that confirms our preexisting beliefs and ignore information that contradicts them. In finance, this can lead to overconfidence in our investment choices or a failure to adequately assess financial risk. To counteract this bias, actively seek out diverse opinions and data, challenging your assumptions and decisions.

This bias leads us to overestimate our knowledge, ability, and control over financial outcomes. It manifests in various ways, from trading stocks too frequently (and incurring unnecessary fees and losses) to underestimating the risks of financial ventures. Combating overconfidence requires humility, ongoing education, and sometimes, a healthy dose of skepticism about our financial prowess.

Humans tend to prefer avoiding losses to acquiring equivalent gains. This fear of loss can paralyze decision-making, preventing us from taking calculated risks necessary for financial growth. It can also lead to holding onto losing investments for too long, hoping to "break even." Recognizing loss aversion in ourselves can help us make more balanced decisions, weighing potential gains against losses in a more rational manner.

There's safety in numbers, or so our instincts tell us. Herd behavior leads us to follow the financial decisions of the majority, often without independent analysis. This bias can inflate bubbles and exacerbate crashes. To avoid the pitfalls of herd behavior, cultivate a practice of independent research and reflection, making financial decisions based on your own circumstances and goals rather than the prevailing winds of popular opinion.

Mitigating these biases begins with awareness. By understanding the common pitfalls in our thinking, we can adopt strategies to navigate around them. This includes:

- Taking a step back to evaluate decisions from multiple perspectives.
- Seeking the counsel of financial advisors or using financial planning tools to provide objective analysis.
- Embracing a mindset of lifelong learning, recognizing that financial literacy is an ongoing journey.
- Practicing mindfulness in financial decisions, checking in with our motives and the influences on our thinking.

Cognitive biases are not flaws to be ashamed of but aspects of our human nature to be understood and managed. By bringing them into the light, we equip ourselves to make more informed, rational financial decisions, paving the way for a more secure and prosperous financial future.

Creating a Positive Relationship with Money

Cultivating a positive relationship with money is akin to nurturing a healthy relationship with a friend or partner—it requires understanding, respect, and consistent effort. This relationship is foundational to achieving not just financial success, but also personal fulfillment and peace. Here's how you can begin this transformative journey:

Every individual has a unique "money story," a narrative composed of past experiences, lessons learned, and beliefs formed about money. Reflecting on your money story is the first step towards rewriting it. Ask yourself:

- What are my earliest memories of money?
- How have my family's attitudes toward money influenced me?
- What positive or negative experiences have shaped my financial beliefs?

Answering these questions can uncover deep-seated beliefs that may be hindering your financial progress. Awareness is the precursor to change.

Gratitude shifts our focus from what we lack to what we possess. Start by appreciating the financial resources you have and the opportunities they provide. This mindset shift can dramatically alter your financial decisions, encouraging you to make choices from a place of abundance rather than scarcity.

A positive relationship with money includes setting and respecting boundaries. This means learning to say no to unnecessary spending, establishing limits, and making conscious choices about how you use your money. Boundaries protect your financial well-being, allowing you to pursue your long-term goals with integrity and purpose.

Knowledge is power, especially when it comes to finances. A positive relationship with money is built on a foundation of understanding. Invest time in learning about budgeting, saving, investing, and other financial principles. The more you know, the more empowered you'll feel to make wise financial decisions.

The scarcity mindset sees limitations and obstacles; the abundance mindset sees opportunities and possibilities. Cultivating an abundance mindset involves:

- Recognizing the abundance in your life, not just in financial terms but in all aspects.
- Believing in your capacity to create and attract more wealth.
- Viewing setbacks as opportunities for growth and learning.

Financial well-being isn't just about the numbers in your bank account; it's about how those numbers impact your life and happiness. It means making financial decisions that align with your values, goals, and what truly brings you joy. This alignment ensures that your finances support your overall well-being, rather than detract from it.

Positive relationships are built on consistent, positive actions. Developing healthy financial habits—such as regular saving, mindful spending, and strategic investing—is key. These habits not only improve your financial health but also reinforce your positive relationship with money.

Just as in personal relationships, it's okay to seek support in your relationship with money. This could be in the form of financial advisors, supportive friends or family members, or communities that share your financial goals. Support can provide encouragement, advice, and accountability, helping you navigate your financial journey.

Recognize and celebrate your financial achievements, no matter how small. Celebrating milestones reinforces your positive relationship with money and motivates you to continue on your path. It's a way of acknowledging your progress and honoring the effort you've put into achieving financial health.

Self-Reflection Questions

1. **Reflect on Your Money Story**: What are the most impactful memories or lessons about money from your childhood, and how do they influence your financial decisions today? Consider both positive and negative influences and their roots in your past.

_____

_____

_____

_____

_____

2. **Identify Your Cognitive Biases**: Can you recognize any cognitive biases in your financial decision-making process? Think about recent financial decisions and analyze them for signs of biases such as overconfidence, loss aversion, or herd behavior.

3. **Assess Your Relationship with Money**: How would you describe your current relationship with money? Is it one of fear, control, scarcity, or abundance? Reflect on what has led to this relationship and how it affects your financial well-being.

4. **Consider Your Financial Boundaries**: What financial boundaries have you set for yourself, if any? Are you able to maintain them, or do you find yourself frequently crossing these lines? Reflect on the reasons behind your actions and how you can reinforce these boundaries.

_____

_____

_____

_____

_____

5. **Envision Your Financial Well-being:** What does financial well-being look like to you? Consider not just the quantitative aspects, such as savings or debt levels, but also how you want to feel about your finances and the role you want money to play in your life.

_____

_____

_____

_____

Chapter Summary

This chapter delves into the profound impact our mindset and psychological biases have on our financial decisions and overall relationship with money. It begins by exploring how our financial mindset, shaped by early experiences and societal influences, dictates our approach to money management, risk-taking, and goal setting. The journey through this chapter illuminates the often unconscious cognitive biases that skew our financial decisions, including anchoring, confirmation bias, overconfidence, loss aversion, and herd behavior. By bringing these biases into the light, the chapter empowers readers to recognize and mitigate their influence, paving the way for more rational and beneficial financial choices.

Moving beyond the identification of biases, the chapter offers a transformative path towards cultivating a positive relationship with money. It emphasizes the importance of understanding one's money story, practicing gratitude, setting clear financial boundaries, embracing education, and fostering a mindset of abundance. The chapter provides actionable strategies for developing healthy financial habits, seeking support, and celebrating financial milestones, all aimed at achieving financial well-being that aligns with one's values and life goals.

Through a blend of psychological insight, practical advice, and reflective exercises, this chapter guides readers on a journey of self-discovery and transformation. It challenges readers to confront and reshape their financial paradigms, ultimately leading to a more empowered, informed, and positive engagement with their finances. The self-reflection questions at the end of the chapter are designed to deepen the reader's understanding of their own financial behaviors and to encourage a proactive approach to financial health and happiness.

Chapter 3: The Vision of Prosperity

"Prosperity does not happen by chance; it is created by the choices we make."

In a world where financial narratives are often dominated by tales of overnight success and catastrophic failures, the true essence of financial prosperity remains shrouded in mystery for many. Yet, at its core, prosperity is not a destination but a journey—one that begins with a clear vision and is sustained by deliberate, purposeful action. This chapter is dedicated to unraveling the fabric of this journey, guiding you towards a personalized definition of financial success, setting goals that resonate with your deepest aspirations, and harnessing the power of visualization and affirmations to turn your financial dreams into reality.

Defining What Financial Success Looks Like for You

Financial success is a concept as diverse as humanity itself. For some, it might mean the freedom to travel the world without financial constraints; for others, it could signify the ability to support their family's needs without worry. The first step toward achieving financial prosperity is to define what success means to you, personally. This definition is your North Star, guiding every decision, every sacrifice, and every triumph on your path to financial wellbeing.

Begin by asking yourself what truly matters to you. Is it security, freedom, the ability to give generously, or perhaps a mix of these? Reflect deeply on your life's priorities and how they align with your financial aspirations. This exercise is not about societal expectations or external benchmarks of wealth; it's about what brings you joy, fulfillment, and a sense of achievement.

Your values are the compass that guides your journey to financial success. Identifying these values helps ensure that your financial goals are not just about accumulating wealth but about creating a life that is rich in meaning and satisfaction. Whether it's the value of independence, education, family, or creativity, understanding what you stand for is crucial in painting a picture of your ideal financial future.

Setting SMART Financial Goals

Once you've defined what financial success looks like for you, the next step is to translate this vision into actionable goals. SMART goals—Specific, Measurable, Achievable, Relevant, and Time-bound—provide a framework that transforms vague aspirations into concrete targets.

Vague goals are the graveyard of progress. A goal that's clearly defined provides a direct path to follow. Instead of "I want to be rich," a specific goal would say, "I aim to have $50,000 saved for a down payment on a house in three years."

A goal must be measurable to assess progress. Determine the metrics that will indicate you're moving in the right direction. If your goal is to improve your investment portfolio, decide on the benchmarks that will reflect success, such as achieving a certain rate of return or reaching a specific portfolio value.

Goals should stretch your abilities but remain within the realm of possibility. Setting an unachievable goal is a recipe for disappointment and demotivation. Assess your resources, skills, and time frame, and set goals that are challenging yet attainable.

Every goal should be relevant to your overarching vision of financial success. This alignment ensures that every effort you put forth contributes directly to the life you envision for yourself. It's about making sure that the ladder you're climbing is leaning against the right wall.

A deadline serves as a powerful motivator. It creates a sense of urgency and helps prioritize actions. By setting a time frame for your goals, you're committing to a timeline for action, which can significantly accelerate your journey to financial success.

The Importance of Visualization and Affirmations in Achieving Financial Success

The power of the mind in manifesting financial prosperity cannot be overstated. Visualization and affirmations are tools that leverage this power, transforming your mindset and aligning your subconscious with your financial aspirations.

Visualization is not mere daydreaming; it is a practice backed by science. When you visualize achieving your financial goals, you activate the same neural networks that are involved in the actual performance of those achievements. This process, known as the "mental rehearsal," enhances motivation, increases confidence, and improves decision-making, thereby making your goals feel attainable.

Effective visualization involves more than just picturing success; it's about creating a vivid, multi-sensory experience in your mind's eye. Imagine not only the visual details of your success but also the sounds, the emotions, and the sense of achievement that accompanies it. Regular practice of this visualization can significantly impact your mindset and actions, propelling you towards your goals.

Affirmations are positive statements that, when repeated regularly, reinforce your goals and boost your self-belief. By affirming your ability to achieve your financial goals, you are programming your subconscious to identify opportunities, solutions, and actions that support your aspirations.

Your affirmations should be personal, positive, present tense, and powerful. For example, "I am confidently making wise financial decisions that lead me to prosperity." Repeat your affirmations daily, and with conviction, to embed these beliefs deep within your subconscious, shaping your thoughts and actions in alignment with your financial goals.

In this chapter, we have embarked on a journey to define, detail, and drive towards your vision of prosperity. Through the thoughtful definition of what financial success means to you, the strategic setting of SMART financial goals, and the empowering practice of visualization and affirmations, you are not just dreaming of a prosperous future; you are actively constructing the road map to achieve it. This is the essence of the vision of prosperity—a vision that is uniquely yours and within your power to realize.

Self-Reflection Questions

1. What does financial success truly mean to you? Reflect on your personal values and how they align with your vision of financial success. Consider what aspects of your life would change with this success and how it would impact your sense of fulfillment and happiness.

2. Are your financial goals SMART? Take a moment to evaluate your current financial goals. Are they specific, measurable, achievable, relevant, and time-bound? If not, how can you adjust them to fit these criteria better?

_____

_____

_____

_____

_____

3. How often do you practice visualization, and what does your vision of financial success look like? Reflect on the clarity, frequency, and emotional intensity of your visualization practices. Are you able to vividly picture your goals and the steps you are taking to achieve them?

_____

_____

_____

_____

4. What affirmations can you create to support your journey towards financial prosperity? Think about positive, present tense statements that resonate with your financial aspirations. How can these affirmations be integrated into your daily routine to reinforce your mindset shift?

5. In what ways can you align your daily actions with your long-term financial vision? Consider the small, daily decisions and habits that contribute to or detract from your financial goals. How can you make more aligned choices moving forward?

Chapter Summary

In Chapter 3, "The Vision of Prosperity," we've embarked on a transformative journey, exploring the foundations of financial success through the lenses of personal definition, goal setting, and the power of the mind. This chapter serves as a cornerstone, laying out the essential steps for anyone looking to redefine their financial future.

We began by understanding that financial success is a deeply personal concept, shaped by individual values and life aspirations. Recognizing that each person's vision of prosperity is unique, we delved into the importance of defining what financial success means to you. This personal definition acts as a guiding star, illuminating the path toward achieving your financial dreams.

The conversation then transitioned to the practicalities of goal setting, emphasizing the significance of SMART (Specific, Measurable, Achievable, Relevant, Time-bound) goals. This framework is crucial for transforming abstract dreams into tangible targets, providing clear direction and milestones for your financial journey.

Further enriching this pathway, we explored the transformative power of visualization and affirmations. These tools not only nurture a positive financial mindset but also align your subconscious with your goals, enhancing motivation and the ability to recognize opportunities. Effective visualization involves creating vivid, multi-sensory experiences of your financial success, while affirmations reinforce your commitment and capability to achieve your objectives.

Through introspective self-reflection questions, readers are encouraged to engage deeply with their financial aspirations, evaluate their current strategies, and embrace practices that foster a prosperity-oriented mindset. This chapter is designed not only to inform but to inspire action, guiding readers to manifest their vision of financial success into reality.

Chapter 4: Strategies for Shifting Your Money Mindset

"Money is a tool. Used wisely, it creates magic. Used poorly, it turns to dust."

In the journey towards financial freedom and abundance, understanding the mechanics of money management, saving, and investing is undoubtedly important. Yet, the bedrock of true financial transformation lies deeper, in the realms of our beliefs, habits, and attitudes towards money—our money mindset. This chapter delves into the psychological underpinnings of our financial lives, presenting strategies not just to alter, but to fundamentally shift your money mindset towards prosperity and growth.

The path to reshaping your financial destiny begins with the mind. It's in the mind that we harbor our deepest fears, nurture our greatest dreams, and conceive the plans that will lead us to our destinies. Therefore, transforming our financial reality must start with changing how we think about and interact with money. This chapter is designed to guide you through this transformative process, focusing on three pivotal strategies: Mindfulness and Money, Overcoming Limiting Beliefs About Wealth, and Cultivating a Growth Mindset Towards Money.

Mindfulness and Money: Staying Present with Your Financial Decisions

In a world where distractions are at our fingertips, staying present and mindful about our financial decisions has become more crucial than ever. Mindfulness in finance is about bringing a heightened state of awareness to our financial behaviors and decisions. It's about making conscious choices rather than reactive ones, understanding the why behind our spending, and aligning our financial actions with our deepest values and goals.

Mindfulness starts with awareness. It's about observing our financial behaviors without judgment. Begin by tracking your spending for a month, not with the goal to criticize or change immediately, but to simply observe. This act of observation is powerful—it illuminates patterns and reveals the emotional triggers behind our spending habits.

With awareness comes the ability to make more intentional choices. Before making a purchase, ask yourself, "Is this in alignment with my financial goals? Does it bring me closer to the life I want to lead?" This practice of pausing and reflecting before spending can transform impulsive buying into thoughtful investing in your future.

Saving, when approached mindfully, is not a restriction but a form of self-care. Viewing saving as a way to honor your future self can shift it from a chore to a deeply fulfilling practice. Create savings goals that resonate with your values and vision for your life, making the act of saving a joyful affirmation of your future dreams.

Overcoming Limiting Beliefs About Wealth

Our financial reality is often a reflection of our inner beliefs about money. Many of us carry limiting beliefs that unconsciously sabotage our financial growth. These beliefs may stem from childhood, societal messages, or past failures. Overcoming them is essential for creating a new financial identity.

The first step is to identify your limiting beliefs. These might be thoughts like "Money is the root of all evil," "I don't deserve to be wealthy," or "I'll never be good with money." Recognize these as stories you've told yourself, not immutable truths.

Once identified, challenge these beliefs. Ask yourself, "Is this belief absolutely true? How does it serve me? What new belief could empower me instead?" Replacing a limiting belief with an empowering one is a process of constant affirmation and evidence gathering. For every limiting belief, create a counterstatement that is positive and affirming, and look for evidence in your life that supports this new belief.

Visualization and affirmation are powerful tools for embedding new beliefs into your subconscious. Regularly visualize yourself achieving your financial goals, experiencing the feelings of success, freedom, and security. Pair this visualization with affirmations that reinforce your new, empowering beliefs about money.

Cultivating a Growth Mindset Towards Money

A growth mindset, the belief that your abilities and intelligence can be developed over time, is foundational to financial success. It's about seeing challenges as opportunities for growth, learning from failures, and persisting in the face of setbacks.

View every financial challenge as an opportunity to learn and grow. Whether it's a budget that didn't work out, an investment that didn't pay off, or a job loss, each challenge holds valuable lessons. Embrace these lessons, adjust your strategies, and move forward with renewed determination.

Incorporate the word "yet" into your financial vocabulary. Instead of saying, "I'm not good at saving," say, "I'm not good at saving yet." This small linguistic tweak can make a significant difference in how you perceive your ability to grow financially.

Commit to being a lifelong learner in the realm of personal finance. Read books, attend workshops, and seek advice from those more experienced. The landscape of personal finance is ever-evolving, and staying informed and adaptable is key to cultivating a growth mindset towards money.

As we delve deeper into each of these strategies in the following sections, remember that shifting your money mindset is a journey, not a destination. It's a process of continuous self-discovery, learning, and growth. Your financial transformation begins in the mind, and with each step forward, you're not just moving towards greater financial freedom—you're creating a richer, more abundant life in every sense.

Self-Reflection Questions

1. **Mindfulness and Money:** Reflect on a recent financial decision you made impulsively. What emotions or circumstances led to that decision? How might you approach a similar situation differently using mindfulness?

2. **Overcoming Limiting Beliefs About Wealth**: Identify one limiting belief about money that you hold. Trace its origin— where did this belief come from? How has it influenced your financial behavior, and what steps can you take to challenge and replace it with an empowering belief?

_____

_____

3. **Cultivating a Growth Mindset Towards Money**: Think of a financial challenge you've recently faced. What did you learn from this experience? How can you apply this lesson to future financial decisions to foster a growth mindset?

_____

_____

_____

_____

_____

4. **Intentional Spending**: Consider your spending habits over the past month. Identify one purchase that aligned perfectly with your values and one that did not. What does this tell you about your financial priorities, and how can you make more aligned decisions moving forward?

_____

_____

_____

5. **Visualization and Affirmation**: Create a vivid mental image of your ideal financial future. What does it look like, and how does it feel to be there? Craft an affirmation that encapsulates this vision. How will you integrate this affirmation into your daily routine to keep your goals and beliefs aligned?

Chapter Summary

Chapter 4, "Strategies for Shifting Your Money Mindset," serves as a comprehensive guide to fundamentally transforming how you perceive, interact with, and grow your wealth. This transformation is pivotal, not just for achieving financial success, but for fostering a life enriched with abundance, freedom, and peace of mind.

The journey begins with Mindfulness and Money, emphasizing the importance of staying present with your financial decisions. This section equips you with strategies to practice intentional spending and saving, urging you to make financial choices that resonate with your deepest values and goals.

Next, we tackle Overcoming Limiting Beliefs About Wealth, a crucial step for anyone looking to break free from the invisible shackles that hinder financial growth. By identifying, challenging, and replacing limiting beliefs with empowering ones, you pave the way for a renewed financial identity grounded in abundance and possibility.

Cultivating a Growth Mindset Towards Money shifts the focus to resilience, learning, and adaptability. Embracing challenges, incorporating the power of "yet," and committing to continuous learning are highlighted as key strategies for fostering a mindset that views financial growth as a journey of endless potential and opportunity.

Throughout the chapter, you're encouraged to engage deeply with self-reflection questions designed to personalize your journey. These questions are not just exercises but invitations to dive into the depths of your financial psyche, challenging you to confront and reshape the beliefs and behaviors that define your financial life.

By integrating the strategies outlined in this chapter, you're not merely changing how you manage money; you're embarking on a transformative journey towards a richer, more fulfilling life. This chapter provides the tools and insights needed to shift your money mindset from one of scarcity and fear to one of growth, abundance, and empowerment, setting the stage for a financial transformation that transcends the numbers in your bank account.

Chapter 5: Building Your Financial Knowledge Base

"An investment in knowledge pays the best interest." - Benjamin Franklin

In the realm of personal finance, knowledge is more than power—it's the engine that drives your journey towards financial independence and prosperity. Building your financial knowledge base is akin to constructing a sturdy foundation for your future; without it, your aspirations and dreams remain on shaky ground. This chapter is dedicated to transforming you from a passive participant in your financial story to an empowered architect of your wealth.

We live in a world where the complexity of financial instruments and the volatility of markets can seem daunting. Yet, the essence of financial mastery lies in understanding and leveraging three foundational pillars: budgeting, saving, and investing. These are not mere activities but profound skills that, when mastered, can turn the tide of your financial destiny.

Basic Financial Literacy: Budgeting, Saving, and Investing

Imagine building a house without a blueprint. Budgeting is the blueprint for building your financial house, one that withstands the test of time and uncertainty. It's about understanding the inflow and outflow of your money, enabling you to make informed decisions that align with your financial goals.

The key to effective budgeting lies in its simplicity and adaptability. Start by tracking your income and expenses, categorizing them to understand where your money is going. Tools and apps can streamline this process, but the goal is to create a system that works for you, one that you can stick to consistently.

The 50/30/20 rule is a simple yet powerful budgeting guideline: 50% of your income goes to needs, 30% to wants, and 20% towards savings and debt repayment. This framework is not rigid; adjust it to fit your unique financial situation and goals.

Saving is the art of withholding today's resources for tomorrow's dreams. It's a testament to your self-discipline and commitment to your future self. Yet, saving is not merely about putting money aside; it's about doing so wisely.

Emergency funds are a critical component of a robust saving strategy, offering a financial lifeline when unforeseen circumstances arise. Aim to save at least three to six months' worth of living expenses. Beyond emergency savings, set specific goals—whether it's for a down payment on a home, a dream vacation, or retirement—and tailor your saving strategy to meet them.

If saving is about preservation, investing is about multiplication. Investing is how you turn your saved money into a wealth-generating engine. The key to successful investing is understanding your risk tolerance and investment horizon. Start with the basics: stocks, bonds, mutual funds, and ETFs. Diversification is your best defense against risk—a diversified portfolio can weather market volatility and yield returns over the long term.

Remember, investing is not a get-rich-quick scheme but a disciplined approach to growing your wealth over time. Educate yourself, start small, and consider seeking advice from financial professionals to navigate the complex world of investing.

Understanding the Power of Compound Interest

Albert Einstein reportedly called compound interest "the eighth wonder of the world." He who understands it, earns it; he who doesn't, pays it. Compound interest is the engine of wealth creation, a force so powerful that it can transform modest savings into substantial sums over time.

The magic of compound interest lies in its ability to earn interest on interest, creating a snowball effect. The earlier you start saving and investing, the more time your money has to grow through compounding. For example, if you invest $10,000 at an annual interest rate of 7%, in 30 years, you wouldn't have merely doubled your money; you'd have over $76,000.

To leverage the power of compound interest, start investing as early as possible. Even small, regular contributions can grow significantly over time. Automate your savings and investments to ensure you're consistently contributing, and reinvest your returns to maximize the compounding effect.

Navigating the World of Credit Wisely

Credit can be a double-edged sword. Used wisely, it can be a powerful tool to build your financial future; used imprudently, it can lead to a cycle of debt that hampers your financial progress. Understanding how to navigate the world of credit is crucial for maintaining a healthy financial life.

First, understand the basics of credit scores and how they affect your ability to borrow and the interest rates you're offered. Paying bills on time, keeping credit card balances low, and avoiding unnecessary debt are key strategies for maintaining a strong credit score.

When using credit cards, treat them as tools for convenience and rewards, not as extensions of your income. Pay off your balances in full each month to avoid interest charges and debt accumulation. For loans, whether it's for a car, education, or a home, ensure that the repayments fit comfortably within your budget and that the terms are favorable.

In the world of credit, knowledge and discipline are your best allies. By understanding and applying the principles of credit wisely, you can use it to your advantage without falling into the trap of debt.

Self-Reflection Questions

1. **Budgeting**: Reflect on your current budgeting practices. Are they effective in helping you manage your finances, or do they need adjustment? Consider how closely you adhere to your budget and whether it aligns with your financial goals.

---

2. **Saving**: Evaluate your savings habits. Do you have an emergency fund, and if so, is it sufficient to cover 3-6 months of living expenses? Think about what saving goals you have set for yourself and how committed you are to achieving them.

---

3. **Investing**: Assess your understanding of and comfort with investing. Are you actively investing, or is it an area you've avoided due to uncertainty or fear? Contemplate what steps you could take to improve your investment knowledge and strategies.

4. **Compound Interest**: Reflect on your current use of compound interest. Do you have investments or savings accounts that leverage compound interest to grow over time? Consider how you might better utilize compound interest to enhance your financial growth.

5. Credit: Think about your relationship with credit. Are you using credit wisely, or do you find yourself struggling with debt? Reflect on how you can improve your credit habits to strengthen your financial situation.

Chapter Summary

In Chapter 5, "Building Your Financial Knowledge Base," we embarked on a comprehensive exploration of the foundational elements essential for achieving financial literacy and independence. This journey began with understanding the critical importance of budgeting, saving, and investing—three pillars that serve as the bedrock for sound financial management and growth.

Budgeting was introduced as the blueprint for financial success, a tool to meticulously plan and monitor income and expenditures. We discussed the significance of adopting a simple, adaptable budgeting framework, like the 50/30/20 rule, to ensure financial decisions align with personal goals and needs.

Moving on to saving, the chapter highlighted the discipline of setting aside resources for future use, emphasizing the creation of an emergency fund as a safety net. We explored setting specific saving goals and adopting strategies to achieve them, reinforcing the concept that saving is a foundational step towards financial security.

Investing was portrayed as the vehicle for wealth creation, with a focus on starting early, understanding risk tolerance, and diversifying investments to harness the power of the market for long-term financial growth. The chapter demystified the basics of investing, encouraging readers to see it as an accessible and essential component of their financial strategy.

The transformative power of compound interest was unveiled, illustrating how it works to exponentially increase wealth over time. By emphasizing early and consistent investment, the chapter underscored compound interest as a crucial element in the wealth-building equation.

Lastly, navigating the world of credit wisely was discussed, teaching readers how to use credit to their advantage while avoiding the pitfalls of debt. The chapter provided practical advice on managing credit scores, using credit cards responsibly, and understanding the terms of loans.

This chapter aimed to empower readers with the knowledge and tools necessary to take control of their financial destiny. By building a solid financial knowledge base, readers are equipped to make informed decisions, utilize financial instruments to their advantage, and set a course toward financial freedom and prosperity.

Chapter 6: Money Management Mastery

"Control your finances, or they will control you." - A principle echoed through the halls of financial wisdom.

Diving into the heart of financial transformation, Chapter 6 beckons us into the realm of Money Management Mastery—a pivotal juncture where theory meets action, where knowledge crystallizes into tangible results. This chapter is not merely about understanding money; it's about commanding it, shaping it into a tool that carves the path to your dreams.

Creating a Winning Financial Plan

My journey to mastering money management began on a brisk autumn evening. Seated at my aged oak desk, surrounded by piles of bills and faded receipts, a realization dawned upon me: My finances were a reflection of a ship adrift at sea, at the mercy of the wind's whims. It was time to seize the helm.

The creation of a winning financial plan is akin to drawing a map for a treasured expedition. It starts with knowing your current location—your income, expenses, debts, and savings. I meticulously listed every financial detail, no matter how small, confronting the reality of my situation.

The next step was charting the course—setting clear, achievable financial goals. These weren't mere wishes cast into the night sky but lighthouses guiding my journey. From paying off debt to saving for a house, each goal was a beacon of hope.

But how does one navigate the tumultuous waters of unexpected expenses and economic downturns? The answer lay in flexibility. My financial plan was not a rigid cage but a living document, adaptable to the changing tides of life.

In sharing my story, I extend a hand to you, the reader. Begin by assessing your financial landscape. Set goals that spark a fire in your heart. And remember, flexibility is the compass that will guide you through storms.

Effective Budgeting Techniques for Wealth Accumulation

If creating a financial plan is drawing the map, then budgeting is the act of walking the path, one step at a time. My initial attempts at budgeting were akin to a novice sailor trying to tame the sea— filled with enthusiasm but lacking direction.

The breakthrough came when I embraced the 50/30/20 rule—a simple yet powerful budgeting technique. Fifty percent of my income was allocated to necessities, thirty percent to wants, and twenty percent to savings and debt repayment. This structure was my North Star, keeping me aligned with my financial goals.

But the true art of budgeting lies in customization. I learned to tweak the percentages based on my unique financial situation and goals. When I aimed to accelerate my debt repayment, I adjusted the allocations, increasing the percentage towards debt and reducing the allocation for wants.

Budgeting became a game of strategy, where every dollar had a purpose, every expense was scrutinized, and savings were not mere leftovers but a priority. The discipline forged in the fires of budgeting was the cornerstone of my wealth accumulation.

To you, embarking on this journey, I say: Find a budgeting technique that resonates with your soul. Embrace it, adapt it, and watch as the seeds of your discipline bloom into the garden of wealth.

Emergency Funds and Financial Security

The final piece of the Money Management Mastery puzzle is the creation of an emergency fund—a financial safety net that catches you when the ground beneath you crumbles. My initiation into the importance of emergency funds came through a trial by fire—a sudden job loss that left me staring into the abyss of uncertainty.

The conventional wisdom of saving three to six months' worth of expenses seemed a Herculean task. Yet, the peace of mind it promised was a beacon in the storm. Starting small, I redirected a portion of my savings into an emergency fund, gradually building it up.

The emergency fund transformed from a concept into a pillar of my financial security, a buffer against the slings and arrows of outrageous fortune. It was not just about having the funds but about the freedom and peace it granted me—the ability to make decisions from a place of strength rather than desperation.

To those standing at the threshold of this realization, know this: The path to financial security is paved with patience and persistence. Start your emergency fund today, no matter how small the contribution. Let it be the bedrock upon which your financial house stands unshakable.

Self-Reflection Questions

1. **Assess Your Financial Landscape**: Where do you currently stand financially? Consider your income, expenses, debts, and savings. Reflect on how this starting point aligns with where you wish to be. What are the most immediate changes you recognize need to be made?

_____

_____

_____

_____

_____

2. **Define Your Financial Goals**: What are your short-term and long-term financial goals? Are they clearly defined, realistic, and aligned with your values and aspirations? How do these goals motivate your daily financial decisions?

_____

_____

_____

_____

_____

3. **Evaluate Your Budgeting Strategy**: How effective is your current budgeting technique? Does it reflect the 50/30/20 rule, or have you adapted a different strategy that better suits your lifestyle and goals? Reflect on the purpose each dollar serves in your budget.

_____

_____

_____

_____

_____

4. **Consider Your Emergency Fund**: Do you have an emergency fund in place? If so, does it cover three to six months of expenses, or are you working towards that goal? Reflect on how having or lacking this fund affects your sense of financial security.

_____

_____

_____

_____

_____

5. **Reflect on Your Journey to Mastery**: Considering the principles of Money Management Mastery discussed, what steps have you taken that demonstrate your progress toward financial mastery? Where do you see room for improvement, and what are the next actions you plan to take?

_____

_____

_____

_____

_____

Chapter Summary

In Chapter 6, "Money Management Mastery," we embarked on an essential journey through the core aspects of mastering one's finances, detailed through a personal narrative that brings the principles to life. This chapter delves into creating a winning financial plan, the art of effective budgeting, and the critical role of emergency funds in ensuring financial security.

Creating a Winning Financial Plan unfolds as the foundational step where assessing your current financial situation and setting clear, achievable goals paves the way for a successful financial future. The personal story emphasizes the importance of flexibility in planning, allowing for adjustments as life's circumstances change.

Effective Budgeting Techniques for Wealth Accumulation shifts focus to the day-to-day management of finances. Through the narrative, the 50/30/20 rule is introduced as a guiding principle, alongside the encouragement to customize budgeting strategies to fit personal goals and lifestyles. The sub-chapter champions budgeting as not only a means of controlling spending but as a strategic tool for wealth growth.

Emergency Funds and Financial Security highlights the creation of an emergency fund as a non-negotiable aspect of financial planning. The personal account underscores the fund's significance in providing a safety net that offers peace of mind and stability, even in the face of unexpected financial challenges.

Through these sub-chapters, readers are guided on a journey of self-discovery and empowerment. The narrative style brings financial concepts to life, making the principles of money management accessible and relatable. By the end of the chapter, readers are equipped with the knowledge and motivation to master their finances, transforming their relationship with money from one of stress and uncertainty to one of confidence and control.

This chapter not only provides the tools and strategies needed for financial mastery but also encourages readers to reflect on their financial practices, to ask critical questions of themselves, and to take actionable steps towards a secure and prosperous financial future.

Chapter 7: The Art of Earning More

"Financial growth requires more than just saving; it's about expanding your capacity to earn." - An often-overlooked truth in the journey toward financial freedom.

In our quest for financial liberation, we've dissected the anatomy of spending, saving, and investing. Yet, a pivotal piece of the puzzle remains—boosting your income. This chapter, "The Art of Earning More," is dedicated to unraveling the secrets of enhancing your earning potential. It's a deep dive into the realms of additional income streams, self-investment, and the entrepreneurial spirit, each a beacon guiding you toward the zenith of financial prosperity.

Exploring Additional Income Streams

My journey into exploring additional income streams began on a crisp autumn evening. The realization dawned upon me; my primary job, while stable, was a single thread holding my financial future. The risk of dependence on a singular income source was a gamble I no longer wished to take. This revelation set me on a path of discovery, seeking out the myriad of ways one could supplement their income.

I ventured first into the digital landscape, a realm where opportunities abound for those willing to seek them. Freelance writing, graphic design, and virtual assistance offered gateways to extra income. Each project completed was not just a transaction but a stepping stone, building a portfolio that attracted more work, more income.

Yet, the digital world was but one facet of the possibilities. Real estate investment became a beacon of passive income, turning the dream of earning while I slept into a tangible reality. Rental properties, though demanding initial capital and effort, began to weave a safety net of financial security beneath me.

But it wasn't just about diversifying income; it was about creating a symphony where each stream played its part in harmony. Investing in dividend-yielding stocks, peer-to-peer lending, and creating online courses on areas of my expertise—each venture opened new doors, each door leading to rooms filled with potential wealth.

Investing in Your Skills and Education for Higher Earnings

The epiphany that learning is earning transformed my approach to personal development. It became clear that the investment in skills and education was not an expense but an investment with the highest returns. I embarked on a quest for knowledge, enrolling in courses that promised to elevate my expertise and, consequently, my market value.

Specializing in high-demand skills such as digital marketing, data analysis, and coding, I noticed a significant shift. Opportunities that were once beyond my reach began to gravitate towards me. Negotiations for higher pay became not just a possibility but a reality, as I leveraged my enhanced skill set to ascend the career ladder.

Continued education was not confined to formal settings. The world around us, ever-evolving, is a classroom. Podcasts, webinars, and books became my allies, each offering nuggets of wisdom that enriched my understanding and capability. This relentless pursuit of knowledge not only amplified my earnings but also instilled a profound sense of fulfillment and confidence.

Entrepreneurship and Side Hustles as a Pathway to Wealth

The allure of entrepreneurship captivated me, the promise of turning visions into ventures, a siren call I could not ignore. My foray into entrepreneurship began with a simple idea, a solution to a problem many faced yet overlooked. The journey from conception to realization was fraught with challenges, yet each obstacle surmounted was a testament to the resilience and creativity that entrepreneurship demands.

Side hustles, in parallel, became a playground for experimentation. From e-commerce stores selling bespoke products to consulting services based on my accumulated expertise, each venture was a lesson in business, marketing, and customer service. The thrill of building something from the ground up, of seeing your efforts bear fruit, was unparalleled.

Entrepreneurship and side hustles taught me the importance of persistence, innovation, and the willingness to take calculated risks. They became not just sources of additional income but avenues for personal growth and the realization of my potential.

As I pen down these experiences, it's evident that the art of earning more is not a pursuit of money for money's sake. It's about the growth, the journey, and the transformation that occurs when you step out of your financial comfort zone. It's about harnessing your passions, skills, and the opportunities that lie in wait, ready for those bold enough to seek them.

This chapter is a testament to the power of diversifying your income, investing in yourself, and embracing the entrepreneurial spirit. It's a guide, a mentor, and a friend for those ready to take the leap into a world where financial limitations are but a distant memory, and financial prosperity is a vivid, achievable reality.

Self-Reflection Questions

1. What fears or hesitations do you have about exploring additional income streams, and how can you address them?
Reflect on any mental barriers or uncertainties that may be holding you back from seeking new ways to earn. Consider practical steps to overcome these challenges, whether it's through further research, seeking mentorship, or starting small.

2. In what areas could you invest in your education or skills to increase your earning potential?

Identify specific skills or knowledge areas where an investment could significantly impact your career or income. Think about how you can start this learning journey, be it through online courses, attending workshops, or reading books related to your field.

3. What entrepreneurial idea or side hustle have you thought about but not pursued? What's stopping you?

Contemplate any business ideas or side hustles you've considered in the past. Reflect on the reasons why you haven't moved forward with them and what steps you could take to test or develop these ideas further.

4. How do you currently balance your time between earning, learning, and personal commitments? Where could adjustments be made?

Evaluate how you allocate your time across various activities and responsibilities. Think about whether there's a need to rebalance your priorities to make room for additional income streams or skill development.

5. What does financial freedom mean to you, and how can diversifying your income help achieve it?

Consider your personal definition of financial freedom and the role that increased and diversified income plays in reaching that state. Reflect on how you can align your efforts in earning more with your long-term financial goals.

_____

_____

_____

_____

_____

Chapter Summary

In this pivotal chapter, "The Art of Earning More," we embarked on a comprehensive journey through the landscapes of enhancing one's income. The chapter unfolds with a deep dive into the necessity and strategies for exploring additional income streams, emphasizing the importance of diversification in financial stability and growth. Through personal anecdotes and practical advice, readers are guided through the digital realms of freelancing, the investment potential in real estate, and the passive income opportunities available in the stock market and beyond.

Further, the narrative shifts focus to the paramount importance of investing in oneself—highlighting how education and skill development directly correlate with one's earning potential. Through stories of personal growth and success, the chapter illustrates the transformative power of continuous learning and specialization in high-demand areas, offering a roadmap for readers to elevate their market value and career opportunities.

Transitioning into the entrepreneurial spirit, the chapter celebrates the courage and creativity inherent in starting one's ventures. It presents entrepreneurship and side hustles not just as avenues for financial gain but as platforms for personal expression, innovation, and fulfillment. By sharing the trials and triumphs of navigating the entrepreneurial journey, the chapter serves as both inspiration and practical guide for readers aspiring to carve their paths in the business world.

Across these narratives, the chapter interweaves themes of resilience, strategic risk-taking, and the relentless pursuit of growth, challenging readers to expand their financial horizons. By the end, "The Art of Earning More" stands as a testament to the idea that earning potential is not fixed but a dynamic aspect of one's life that can be cultivated through curiosity, learning, and entrepreneurial action.

Chapter 8: Investing Wisely for Long-Term Growth

"Money is a terrible master but an excellent servant." - P.T. Barnum

Diving into the heart of wise investment was never just about the act of placing capital into promising ventures; it was about transforming those ventures into vehicles that drive us toward the zenith of financial independence and security. My journey into the realms of the stock market, real estate, and various investment vehicles was not merely a pursuit of wealth—it was a quest for freedom, a path to crafting a future where my financial well-being was secured, and my dreams were no longer just distant wishes but tangible realities waiting to be grasped.

An Introduction to the Stock Market, Real Estate, and Other Investment Vehicles

My adventure began with a foray into the stock market, a vibrant and pulsating arena where fortunes could be made and lost in the blink of an eye. It was here that I learned the value of patience and the power of compounding. Investing in stocks was not about chasing the latest hot tip or attempting to time the market; it was about finding companies with strong fundamentals, visionary leadership, and the potential for long-term growth. It was about becoming part-owners in businesses that aligned with my values and vision for the future.

Real estate presented a different kind of opportunity, one grounded in the tangibility of bricks and mortar. Here, I discovered the allure of passive income through rental properties and the potential for capital appreciation. Real estate investing required a keen eye for location, timing, and market trends, but it offered a unique blend of stability and profitability that was hard to find elsewhere.

Beyond these traditional paths lay a myriad of other investment vehicles, each with its own set of rules, risks, and rewards. From the calculated risks of venture capital and the steady returns of bonds to the innovative world of cryptocurrency and beyond, the landscape was vast and varied. Diving into each of these options was like exploring new territories, each discovery bringing me closer to my ultimate goal of financial freedom.

Risk Management and Diversification

As my journey unfolded, I quickly realized that the thrill of potential gains was always shadowed by the risk of loss. Managing this risk became a cornerstone of my investment philosophy. I learned that risk management was not about avoiding risk altogether but about understanding it, measuring it, and, most importantly, mitigating it.

Diversification emerged as my most trusted ally in this endeavor. By spreading my investments across different asset classes, sectors, and geographies, I was able to create a safety net that protected my portfolio from the volatility of any single investment. Diversification was not just a strategy; it was a principle, a fundamental approach to investing that allowed me to navigate through market ups and downs with confidence and poise.

Building a Portfolio That Reflects Your Financial Goals and Risk Tolerance

The culmination of my investment journey was the creation of a portfolio that was a true reflection of my financial goals, aspirations, and risk tolerance. This was not a one-size-fits-all solution but a personalized strategy that took into account my unique circumstances, my dreams for the future, and my capacity to weather financial storms.

Building this portfolio was an exercise in self-reflection and discipline. It required a deep understanding of my long-term objectives, whether it was retirement planning, wealth accumulation, or leaving a legacy. It also demanded a clear assessment of my risk tolerance, an honest evaluation of how much volatility I was willing to accept in pursuit of my goals.

As I ventured deeper into the art of investing, I was constantly reminded of the delicate balance between risk and reward, between the dreams of today and the realities of tomorrow. My portfolio became a living entity, evolving with my life's changes, responsive to the shifting landscapes of the market, yet always aligned with the core principles that had guided me from the beginning.

In sharing this chapter of my journey, my hope is to illuminate the path for others. Investing wisely for long-term growth is not just about the mechanics of buying and selling or the strategies for risk management and diversification. It's about embarking on a journey of personal and financial growth, a journey that requires patience, discipline, and a steadfast commitment to your vision for the future.

As we delve into the sub-chapters that follow, remember that the essence of wise investing lies not in the accumulation of wealth for its own sake but in the freedom and opportunities that wealth can provide. Let us journey together, exploring the intricate dance of risk and reward, as we build the foundations for a future filled with prosperity, security, and fulfillment.

Self-Reflection Questions

1. **Reflect on Your Financial Goals**: What are your ultimate financial goals, and how do they align with the investment strategies you're currently employing? Consider whether your current portfolio truly reflects these ambitions and what changes might be necessary to better align your investments with your long-term aspirations.

2. **Evaluate Your Risk Tolerance**: How comfortable are you with the level of risk in your investment portfolio? Think about the fluctuations in the market and how you react to them. Does the thought of temporary losses cause you undue stress, or are you comfortable riding out the market's ups and downs for potential long-term gains?

3. **Assess Your Diversification Strategy**: Look at your current investment spread. Do you feel it is sufficiently diversified across different asset classes, sectors, and geographies to protect against volatility? If not, what areas of diversification could you explore further to enhance the stability and growth potential of your portfolio?

_____

_____

_____

_____

4. Consider Your Knowledge and Education: How well do you understand the various investment vehicles available to you, such as the stock market, real estate, bonds, and cryptocurrencies? Are there areas where you could benefit from further education to make more informed investment decisions?

_____

_____

_____

_____

5. Plan for the Future: How does your current investment strategy support your vision for the future? Think about the legacy you wish to leave and the financial security you want to provide for yourself and your loved ones. What steps can you take today to build a portfolio that mirrors these goals?

_____

_____

_____

_____

_____

Chapter Summary

In Chapter 8, "Investing Wisely for Long-Term Growth," we embarked on a comprehensive journey through the realms of the stock market, real estate, and various other investment vehicles, exploring how each can be harnessed to drive us towards the zenith of financial independence and security. The chapter delved into the importance of understanding and managing risk, highlighting diversification as a key strategy for mitigating potential losses and ensuring a stable, growth-oriented portfolio.

We discussed the critical nature of aligning your investment portfolio with your financial goals and risk tolerance, emphasizing the need for a personalized approach that reflects your unique circumstances and aspirations. Through a blend of narrative exploration and practical advice, this chapter aimed to equip you with the knowledge and tools necessary to navigate the complex landscape of investing, empowering you to build a foundation for long-term financial growth.

By reflecting on the self-reflection questions provided, you're encouraged to delve deeper into your financial psyche, evaluating and refining your investment strategies to ensure they are in harmony with your personal goals and risk appetite. This introspective process is crucial for anyone looking to not just navigate the investment world, but to thrive within it, securing a future marked by financial freedom and prosperity.

Chapter 9: Protecting Your Wealth

"An ounce of prevention is worth a pound of cure." - Benjamin Franklin

In the realm of wealth creation, much of our focus is riveted on the accumulation phase: earning more, saving diligently, and investing wisely. Yet, there lies a crucial aspect often overshadowed by the allure of wealth accumulation—protecting your wealth. It's a fundamental principle that securing what you've worked so hard to build is not merely an option but a necessity. This chapter delves into the vital practices of safeguarding your wealth, ensuring that your financial legacy endures the test of time and benefits not just you but future generations.

As we embark on this exploration, I invite you to journey with me through my own experiences and revelations in the realms of insurance, estate planning, tax efficiency, and the stewardship of assets. These components are the bedrock of financial security, acting as the guardians of your wealth against unforeseen adversities.

The Importance of Insurance and Estate Planning

My awakening to the importance of insurance and estate planning came on a day I least expected. I remember sitting across from my financial advisor, who posed a question that struck a chord deep within: "If something were to happen to you tomorrow, what would become of your wealth and your loved ones?" The truth is, like many, I had been so engrossed in building my wealth that I had neglected to protect it.

Insurance, I learned, is not merely a safety net; it's a strategic tool in wealth preservation. It safeguards your financial legacy against the unpredictable waves of life—illness, accidents, and even death. Estate planning, on the other hand, is the blueprint that ensures your wealth transitions according to your wishes, minimizing the burden on your loved ones during challenging times.

I embarked on a quest to understand the intricacies of insurance—life, health, disability, and liability—and how each serves as a pillar in protecting not just me but my family. I delved into the complexities of estate planning, from wills and trusts to power of attorney and healthcare directives. Each step was a revelation, an unveiling of how preparedness could shield my loved ones from unnecessary hardship.

Strategies for Tax Efficiency and Minimizing Liabilities

My journey into the labyrinth of tax efficiency began with a realization during tax season. As I reviewed my financial statements with my accountant, it dawned on me how significant a portion of my wealth was consumed by taxes. It was a pivotal moment that led me to explore strategies for tax minimization.

Tax efficiency is akin to fine-tuning an engine; it's about optimizing your wealth to run smoothly, ensuring that each dollar is leveraged to its fullest potential. I learned about tax-deferred and tax-exempt investment options, how to utilize tax loss harvesting, and the benefits of strategic charitable giving. Each strategy was a piece of the puzzle, helping me to construct a financial plan that minimized liabilities while maximizing growth.

But it wasn't just about the strategies; it was about adopting a proactive mindset towards tax planning. It required regular reviews of my financial plan, staying abreast of tax law changes, and working closely with a tax professional who could guide me through the intricacies of the tax code.

Safeguarding Your Assets for Future Generations

The final cornerstone in protecting your wealth is ensuring its endurance for future generations. This realization hit home during a family gathering, as I listened to the aspirations and dreams of my children and grandchildren. It became clear that my financial legacy was not just about the wealth I would leave behind but about instilling values that would guide my descendants in their own financial journeys.

Safeguarding assets for future generations involves more than just financial planning; it's about legacy planning. It's about creating structures, such as family trusts, that provide not just for your immediate family but for generations to come. It's about educating your heirs on financial stewardship, ensuring they possess the knowledge and values to manage and preserve the family wealth.

I explored various vehicles for passing on wealth, from straightforward beneficiary designations to more complex instruments like dynasty trusts. I engaged in open dialogues with my family about financial values, responsibilities, and the vision for our collective future. This journey was not just about securing financial assets; it was about building a legacy of wisdom, values, and unity.

As we delve deeper into each of these pivotal areas, remember that the essence of protecting your wealth lies in preparation, education, and action. It's a dynamic process, one that requires diligence, foresight, and a commitment to ensuring that your financial legacy stands as a testament to your life's work. Join me as we navigate through the detailed strategies and stories that have not only safeguarded my wealth but also enriched my life and the lives of those I hold dear.

Self-Reflection Questions I

1. **Assess Your Current Protection Strategy**: Have you taken steps to ensure your wealth is protected against unforeseen circumstances? Reflect on whether your current insurance coverage (life, health, disability, and liability) truly aligns with your needs and the needs of your loved ones.

_____

_____

_____

_____

2. Evaluate Your Estate Planning: When was the last time you reviewed your will, trust, or estate plan? Consider if your current estate planning documents accurately reflect your wishes on how your wealth should be distributed and managed in your absence.

3. Consider Tax Efficiency in Your Financial Plan: How tax-efficient is your current investment strategy? Think about whether you are leveraging tax-deferred or tax-exempt investment options and employing strategies like tax loss harvesting to minimize your tax liabilities.

4. Plan for Future Generations: Have you established a clear plan for passing your wealth to future generations? Reflect on whether you have taken steps to not only transfer your wealth but also to impart financial wisdom and values to your heirs.

5. Review Your Asset Protection Measures: Are your assets safeguarded against potential legal liabilities? Consider whether you've implemented strategies such as asset protection trusts or umbrella insurance policies to protect your wealth from lawsuits or creditors.

Chapter Summary

Chapter 9 of "The Winning Money Mindset" book, titled "Protecting Your Wealth," serves as a comprehensive guide to ensuring the longevity and security of your financial legacy. This chapter illuminates the often-overlooked aspects of wealth management, emphasizing the importance of not just accumulating wealth but also protecting it against potential threats.

The chapter begins with a compelling narrative on the awakening to the importance of insurance and estate planning, highlighting how these tools serve as the foundation for safeguarding your financial future and the well-being of your loved ones. Through personal stories and insights, the chapter delves into the various types of insurance coverage and the critical components of a robust estate plan.

Moving on, the narrative shifts to strategies for tax efficiency and minimizing liabilities. Here, the reader is guided through the labyrinth of tax planning, uncovering strategies to optimize their wealth and ensure that their hard-earned money is not unnecessarily eroded by taxes. The chapter emphasizes the significance of a proactive approach to tax planning and the role of professional advice in navigating the complexities of the tax code.

The final part of the chapter focuses on safeguarding assets for future generations, underscoring the importance of legacy planning. Through engaging storytelling, the reader is encouraged to think beyond mere wealth transfer, contemplating the values and lessons they wish to pass along to their heirs. The chapter explores various vehicles for legacy planning and the importance of open family dialogues about financial stewardship.

"Protecting Your Wealth" is a chapter that transcends the traditional financial advice narrative, offering a holistic view of wealth protection. It calls on readers to take a proactive stance in securing their financial legacy, ensuring that their wealth serves not only their own needs but also the needs of future generations. Through a blend of personal reflection, practical strategies, and actionable advice, this chapter equips readers with the knowledge and tools necessary to shield their wealth from unforeseen challenges, thereby ensuring its endurance and impact for years to come.

Chapter 10: Living the Winning Money Mindset

"Financial freedom is a mental, emotional, and educational process." - Robert Kiyosaki.

Embarking on the journey to financial freedom and prosperity is akin to setting sail on the vast, unpredictable ocean of wealth. The key to navigating this journey successfully lies not just in the strength of your ship or the favor of the winds but in the steadfastness of your mindset. The Winning Money Mindset isn't a destination; it's a way of living, a compass by which every financial decision is guided, ensuring your journey is not just prosperous but also purposeful and fulfilling.

Maintaining Your Financial Health

Imagine your financial health as a garden. Just as a garden requires regular care—watering, weeding, and sunlight—so too does your financial health require ongoing attention and nurturing. It's a living entity, affected by the seasons of life, economic climates, and personal growth. To maintain this garden, I've learned to perform regular 'financial check-ups,' a practice akin to weeding, ensuring that my expenses never outgrow my income, and that my savings and investments are always flourishing.

Budgeting is the watering can of this garden, a tool that ensures every dollar, like every drop of water, serves a purpose, nurturing my financial goals towards fruition. I've embraced technology, using apps and spreadsheets not just as tools, but as allies in my quest for financial health, tracking my progress and adjusting my sails as necessary.

Yet, the health of a garden is not measured by its size alone, but by the quality of its soil. In the same way, the health of my finances is not just in the numbers, but in the mindset with which I approach them. Gratitude, rather than greed, has become the soil in which my financial decisions are rooted, transforming my relationship with money from one of scarcity to abundance.

The Role of Philanthropy in Wealth Management

Philanthropy was a concept I once believed was reserved for the end of a successful financial journey, a final act of generosity after achieving personal wealth. However, I've come to understand it as an integral part of wealth management, a practice that enriches not just the lives of others but my own financial well-being.

Incorporating giving into my financial strategy has opened my eyes to the value of money as a tool for impact. It's taught me that wealth is not just for accumulation but for circulation, creating a ripple effect of positivity that extends far beyond my immediate financial circle. This practice has not only brought deeper meaning to my financial goals but has also encouraged me to manage my wealth more effectively, ensuring I have more to give.

Moreover, philanthropy has served as a mirror, reflecting the true value of my financial success. It's challenged me to measure wealth not just by the figures in my bank account but by the difference I make in the world. This shift in perspective has been transformative, instilling a sense of responsibility and purpose in every financial decision I make.

Continuous Learning and Adaptation for Financial Success

The landscape of personal finance is ever-changing, with new opportunities and challenges emerging with the tides of the economy and technology. I've learned that to truly live the Winning Money Mindset, one must be a lifelong learner, constantly seeking new knowledge and adapting to the evolving financial environment.

This journey of continuous learning has taken me beyond the pages of books and into the realms of seminars, online courses, and financial blogs, each a treasure trove of wisdom waiting to be discovered. It's a pursuit fueled by curiosity, a desire to understand the nuances of the market, the intricacies of investment strategies, and the ever-changing tax laws that affect my financial health.

But adaptation is more than just absorbing information; it's about applying this knowledge to my life, experimenting with new strategies, and not being afraid to pivot when circumstances change. This dynamic approach has enabled me to stay ahead, turning potential financial storms into opportunities for growth and learning.

Living the Winning Money Mindset is a journey that never truly ends. It's a commitment to growth, a dedication to purpose, and a celebration of the abundance that life has to offer. As I continue on this path, I am constantly reminded that the true measure of financial success is not in the wealth accumulated but in the lives touched, the dreams achieved, and the legacy left behind.

Self-Reflection Questions

1. How do you currently maintain your financial health, and in what ways could you improve this practice to better support your financial goals?

Reflect on your financial habits, considering both your strengths and weaknesses. Think about how you can enhance your financial health through better budgeting, saving, and investing practices.

2. What role does philanthropy currently play in your life, and how does it reflect your values and financial goals?

Examine your beliefs and actions around giving. Consider how integrating philanthropy into your financial strategy could not only help others but also enrich your own life and align with your broader financial objectives.

_____

_____

_____

3. How do you engage with continuous learning in the realm of personal finance, and what new areas of knowledge could you explore to further your financial success?

Identify the resources and practices you currently use to stay informed about personal finance. Think about new topics or areas within personal finance that you could explore to enhance your understanding and financial well-being.

_____

_____

_____

_____

4. Reflect on a moment when you had to adapt your financial plan in response to an unexpected challenge. What did you learn from this experience, and how has it shaped your approach to financial planning and risk management?

Consider the resilience of your financial planning. Evaluate how past challenges have taught you valuable lessons about adaptability, risk management, and the importance of being prepared for the unexpected.

_____

_____

_____

_____

_____

5. Looking at your financial journey, how does your current mindset align with the Winning Money Mindset, and what steps can you take to further cultivate this mindset?

Assess your current financial mindset in comparison to the ideals and practices outlined in this chapter. Consider practical steps you can take to deepen your understanding of this mindset and integrate its principles more fully into your life.

_____

_____

_____

_____

Chapter Summary

Chapter 10 of "The Winning Money Mindset: Shifting Your Financial Paradigms in a Way That Will Change Your Life" serves as a capstone to the transformative journey outlined in the book. It emphasizes the importance of living the principles of the Winning Money Mindset through three core areas: maintaining financial health, incorporating philanthropy into wealth management, and committing to continuous learning and adaptation for financial success.

Maintaining your financial health is likened to tending a garden, requiring regular attention and care to flourish. The chapter guides readers through practical strategies for budgeting, saving, and investing, all grounded in gratitude and a mindset of abundance.

The role of philanthropy is redefined, not as a final act after achieving wealth but as an integral part of the wealth management process. This section highlights how philanthropy can enrich the giver's life, encouraging readers to view their wealth as a tool for positive impact and to measure success by the difference they make in the world.

Finally, the necessity of continuous learning and adaptation is discussed, underscoring the ever-changing nature of personal finance. The chapter encourages readers to be lifelong learners, open to new knowledge and flexible in their financial strategies, ensuring they can navigate the unpredictable waters of the financial world with confidence.

This chapter, and indeed the entire book, is a call to action for readers to embrace a new way of thinking about money. It's an invitation to embark on a journey of financial transformation that transcends the numbers, touching on the essence of what it means to live a rich, purposeful life. Through self-reflection, practical application, and a commitment to growth, readers are equipped to not only achieve their financial goals but to surpass them, living a life characterized by financial freedom, generosity, and continuous learning.

Conclusion

"Financial freedom is a mental, emotional, and educational process." - Robert Kiyosaki.

As we draw the curtains on this transformative journey with "The Winning Money Mindset," it's important to pause and reflect. This book was never just about financial strategies or managing your money effectively; it was about changing your life. It was about shifting your paradigms and embracing a new financial reality. As you stand on the brink of this new dawn, let's delve deeper into what we've uncovered together and explore how you can carry these lessons into every facet of your life.

My journey began much like yours, with a deep-seated desire for change but a sense of uncertainty about where to start. I remember the days when my financial situation felt like a boat adrift at sea, swayed by every wave, with no land in sight. It was during these times of turmoil that I realized the need for a compass, a guide to navigate through the stormy waters of financial insecurity and into the calm harbors of wealth and abundance. This realization was the seed that grew into "The Winning Money Mindset."

As we embarked on this journey together, we uncovered the layers of financial myths and misconceptions that held us back. We learned that money, at its core, is not just currency but a reflection of our values, beliefs, and decisions. We discovered that the barriers to our financial freedom were not just external but deeply rooted within our mindset and perception.

Through each chapter, we challenged these barriers, armed with knowledge, strategies, and a newfound understanding of wealth. We learned the importance of setting clear, actionable goals and the power of a proactive approach to financial planning. We explored the psychological underpinnings of our relationship with money and how to shift from a mindset of scarcity to one of abundance.

But perhaps the most significant revelation was the realization that our financial journey is intrinsically linked to our personal growth. As we change how we think about and interact with money, we also change how we see ourselves and our potential. This journey was not just about financial transformation but personal transformation.

As we turn the final pages of this book, you may wonder, "What comes next?" The truth is, the end of this book marks the beginning of your real journey. The path ahead is one you will forge with the tools, knowledge, and insights you've gained. It's a path that will require you to apply what you've learned, experiment, and adapt to the unique challenges and opportunities of your financial landscape.

Living beyond the book means taking the principles of "The Winning Money Mindset" and integrating them into your daily life. It means setting and revisiting your financial goals regularly, continuing to educate yourself on financial matters, and staying connected with a community of like-minded individuals who support and inspire your growth.

It also means recognizing that your journey to financial freedom is a marathon, not a sprint. There will be setbacks and challenges along the way, but it's your resilience, perseverance, and commitment to your vision that will carry you through.

Now, I invite you to take a bold step forward. Embrace the new financial paradigm you've uncovered through these pages. This is your moment of transformation, a time to claim ownership of your financial future and the abundance that awaits you.

Remember, the greatest investment you can make is in yourself. Your growth, your education, and your mindset are the keys to unlocking a future of wealth and security. As you move forward, carry with you the lessons of "The Winning Money Mindset" not just as memories but as guiding principles for your life.

Let this book be the foundation upon which you build your dreams, but let your actions and decisions be the bricks and mortar. Challenge yourself to think bigger, to push beyond your comfort zones, and to live with a sense of purpose and possibility.

In closing, I leave you with this thought: Your financial journey is a reflection of your inner journey. As you grow in wisdom, courage, and understanding, so too will your finances reflect this growth in abundance, security, and freedom.

The road ahead is yours to travel, and I have every confidence that you will navigate it with grace, determination, and success. Remember, the mindset you cultivate today will shape your financial reality tomorrow.

This is not the end, dear reader, but a new beginning. Welcome to your new financial paradigm.

THANK YOU PAGE

Dear Esteemed Reader,

As we arrive at the conclusion of this transformative journey together, I find myself reflecting on the path we've ventured down side by side. "The Winning Money Mindset: Shifting Your Financial Paradigms in a Way That Will Change Your Life" was penned with a vision—to light the way for those seeking financial freedom and a deeper understanding of their relationship with money. Your decision to embark on this journey with me has been both an honor and a privilege.

Thank you for investing your time, your trust, and your energy into the pages of this book. Thank you for opening your mind to new perspectives, for challenging your existing beliefs, and for taking bold steps toward reshaping your financial future. Your willingness to explore, question, and apply the principles discussed has not only enriched your path but has also deeply inspired me.

This book was a conversation, a shared exploration of what it means to live with a winning money mindset. Your engagement has transformed this conversation into a vibrant dialogue, one that I hope has brought as much value to your life as your participation has brought to mine.

As you continue on your journey, remember that the transformation you've begun is a continuous process. The shifts in mindset, the strategies learned, and the habits formed are the seeds of a future filled with potential and prosperity. I encourage you to nurture these seeds, to remain curious and committed to your growth, and to always move forward with courage and confidence.

Should you ever find yourself in moments of doubt or uncertainty, let the lessons contained within these pages serve as a beacon, guiding you back to the path of financial empowerment. Remember, the journey to financial freedom is as much about the journey within as it is about the external achievements.

As we part ways in this book, I leave you with my sincerest wishes for your success and happiness. May your life be enriched not just with wealth, but with the joy, peace, and fulfillment that come from living true to your highest potential.

This is not goodbye, but a celebration of the beginning of your new chapter. I look forward to hearing about your successes, learning from your challenges, and continuing to support you in any way I can.

Thank you, once again, for allowing me the privilege to be a part of your journey. Here's to your continued success and to the limitless possibilities that await you.

With deepest gratitude,

Mitchell Larry